To Eric
on his first
Communion day Dec 30, 1973

Bernard

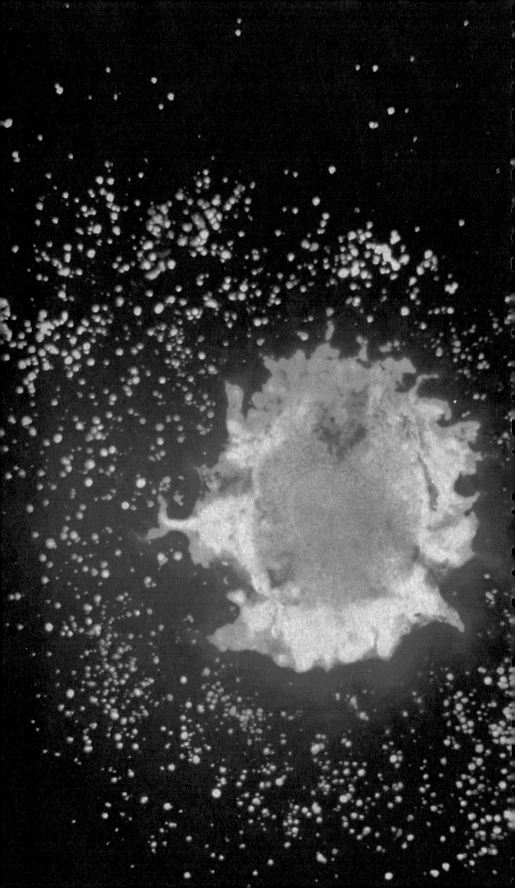

"I'll Make Me a World"

James Weldon Johnson's Story of the Creation

Designed By Jay Johnson

♛ Hallmark Crown Editions

And God stepped out on space,
And He looked around and said:
I'm lonely—
I'll make me a world.

ANO FAR as the eye of God could see
   Darkness
      covered everything...........
Blacker than a hundred midnights
   Down in a cypress swamp...

Then God smiled.....
And the light broke.....
And the darkness rolled up
on one side......
And the light stood shining
on the other......
And God said: *That's good!*

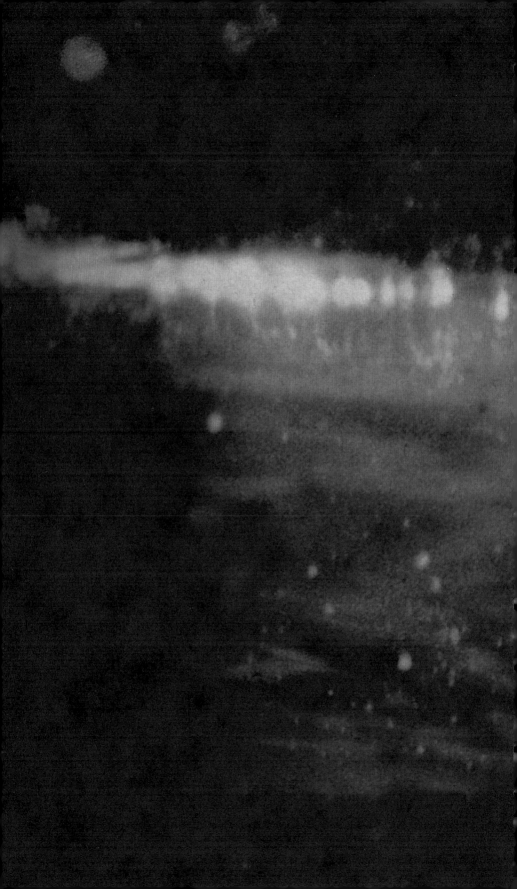

Then God reached out
      and took the light in His hands....
And God rolled the light around in His hands
      Until He made the sun.....
      .....And He set that sun a-blazing
            in the heavens.......

8

Ano the light that was left
      from making the sun…
…God gathered it up in a shining ball
    And flung it
        against the darkness…
…Spangling the night with the moon
        and stars….

11

Then down between
The darkness and the light
        He hurled the world....
        ...And God said: *That's good!*

12

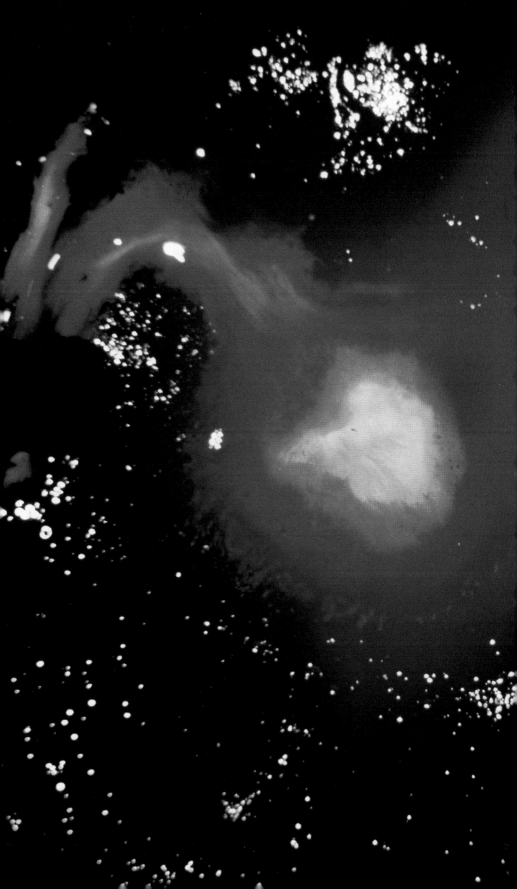

Then God Himself stepped down —
And the sun was on His right hand....
And the moon was on His left....
The stars were clustered about His head.....
And the earth was under His feet....

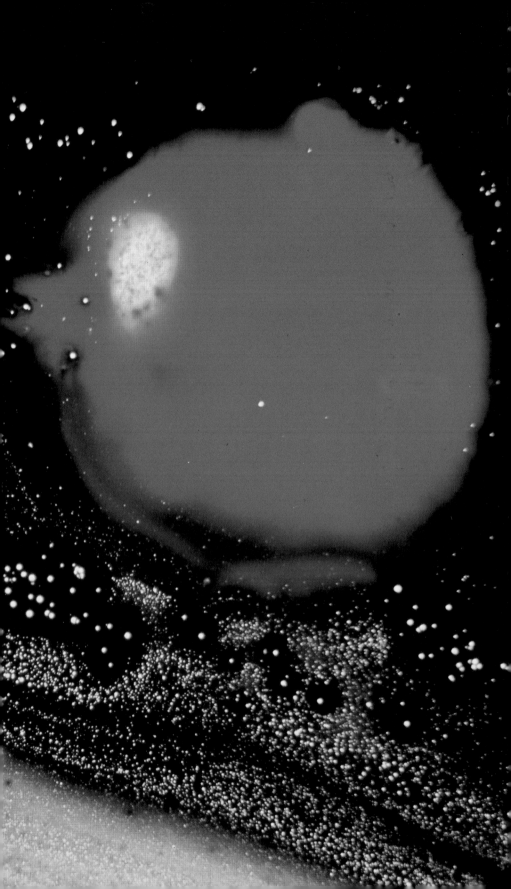

...Anᴅ Goᴅ walked...and where He trod
His footsteps hollowed the valleys out
And bulged the mountains up.....

16

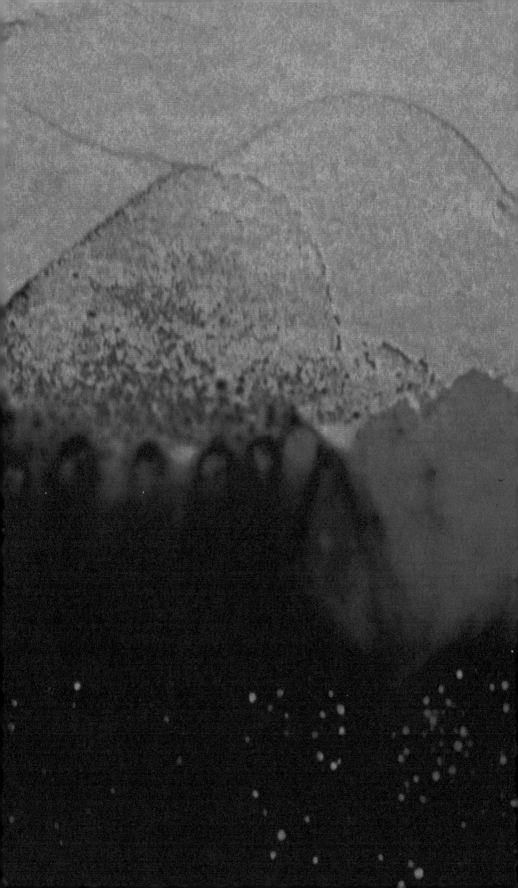

Then He stopped and looked and saw
That the earth was hot
and barren.....

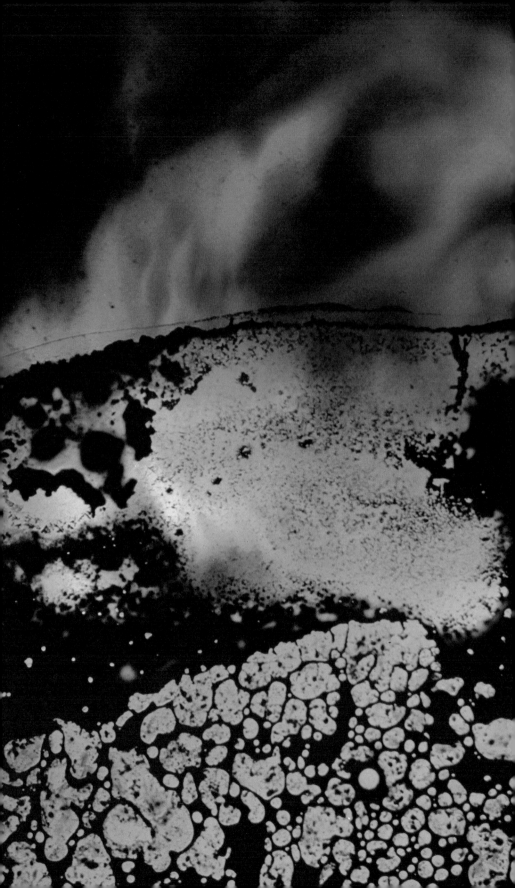

So Gᴏᴅ stepped over
        to the edge of the world
    And He spat out the seven seas—
He batted His eyes, and the lightnings
        flashed....
...He clapped His hands, and the thunders
        rolled.....

21

Anɒ the waters above the earth
        came
            down∴
…The cooling waters
          came down…..

Then the green grass sprouted,
And the little red flowers blossomed.....

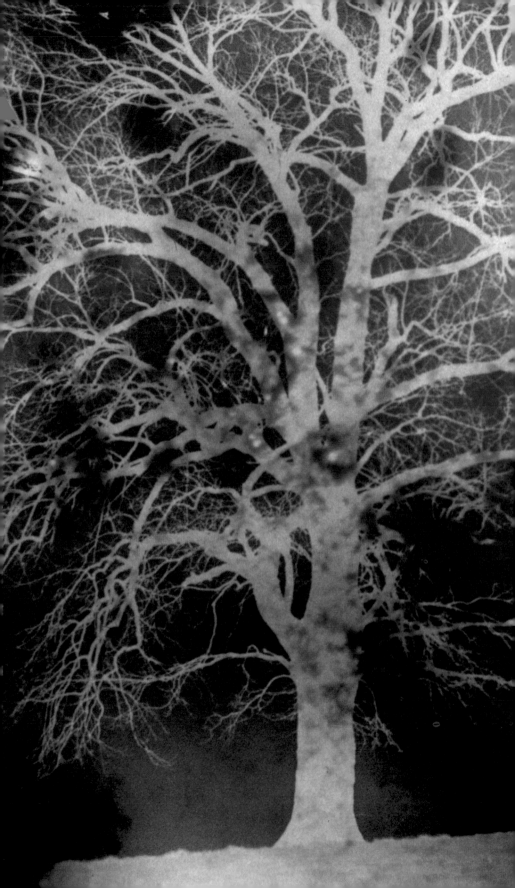

The pine tree pointed his finger
to the sky.....
...And the oak
spread out his arms.....

27

The Lakes cuddled down
in the hollows
of the ground,
The rivers ran down to the sea.....

Anꝺ Goꝺ smiled again.....
...And the rainbow appeared,
And curled itself
around His shoulder.

Then God raised His arm....

...and He waved His hand
Over the sea and over
the land.....

...**And He** said: *Bring forth! Bring forth!*

Aꝺ Quɪcker than God could drop
His hand,
Fishes and fowls...
...And beasts and birds
Swam the rivers and the seas.....
....Roamed the forests and the woods....
...And split the air with their wings.

And God said: *That's good!*

Then God walked around...
        ...And God looked around
On all that He had made.
        He looked at His sun...
...And He looked at His moon....
        ...And He looked at His little stars.....

He Looked on His world
　　With all its living things,
And God said: *I'm lonely still.*

39

Then God sat down....
     ...on the side of a hill
          where He could think...
     ...By a deep, wide river He sat down......
With His head in His hands,
        God thought and thought,
Till He thought...*I'll make me a man!*

up from the bed of the river
God scooped the clay....
...And by the bank of the river
He kneeled Him down...

43

Ano there the great God Almighty...
...Who lit the sun and fixed it
in the sky...
...Who flung the stars
to the most far corner
of the night...
...Who rounded the earth in the middle
of His hand.....

44

This Great God,
    Like a mammy bending over her baby,
    Kneeled down in the dust...

...TOILING OVER a lump of clay
Till He shaped it in His own image...
Then into it He blew the breath
of life....

...And man became a living soul.
Amen. Amen.

Photographers:
Tim Conrad: Pages 4, 6-7, 8-9, 10-11, 13, 14-15, 16-17, C-D,
20, 23, 24, 26-27, 29, 30-31, 32, and Cover
Richard Fanolio: Page 35
Joseph Miurovich: Pages 32-33, 36, 38(D),
38(U), and Endpapers
Mike McCloud: Pages 46-47
David Muench: Pages ... and 40
Plessner International: Page 36-38
Frank Oberle: Pages 34-35, and C
Phil Stoffel: Page 45
Clint Turner: Page 38(C)

Photographic composition and styling by Jim Cozad.
Special photographic techniques were created
by back-lighting transparent dies, oils and crystals.
To achieve the images, the photographer combined
macro-photography and special darkroom techniques.
The type is set in American Uncial, a calligraphic
typeface by Victor Hammer and in Optima,
a sans serif typeface created by Hermann Zapf.
The paper is Hallclear, White Imitation
Parchment and Ivory Fiesta Parchment. The cover is
bound with natural weave book cloth and Torino paper.
Book design by Jay Johnson.

Photographers:
Jim Cozad: Pages A, 6-7, 8-9, 10-11, 13, 14-15, 16-17, C-D,
    20, 22, 24, 26-27, 29, 30-31, 42, and Cover.
Richard Fanolio: Page 39.
Joseph Klemovich: Pages 32-33, 36, 38(LL),
    38(UL), and Endpapers.
Mike McClue: Pages 46-47.
David Muench: Pages 18, and 40.
Plessner International: Pages 34-35.
Fran Rogers: Pages 34-35, and E.
Phil Smith: Page 48.
Gary Turner: Page 38(CL).